# Intriguing Market Manipulations

Written by: Oscar -Oz Benson

Intriguing Market Manipulations

Copyrighted 2013 by Oscar -Oz Benson

Written, Edited and Published by Oscar Benson

## Intriguing Market Manipulations

These pages will show you how to recognize good buys and bad buys. Explained within is why some have been making anywhere from a steady 10 to 20% year after year increase and where some have made ten to hundred baggers (10 to 100 times their original investments) on a consistent basis.

One thing that is extremely important about the American markets is the use of the American dollar. Currently though it does seem to be failing badly and has lost most of its value, however it is still the most favored world currency by many people and in that position offers the best in usage for the market place. This is the premier reason why the US markets continue to come back most of the time. They have the biggest name in the world and that is mostly because the USD has been forced upon most of the countries of the world through the International Monetary Fund (IMF) and the World Bank.

On these pages are found the way to understand more easily the stock market system in the United States and other places around the world so that if you want to, you can take advantage of it to some degree instead of it taking advantage of you entirely.

Investing in Stocks is risky. There are no ways around the risk completely, however with this book you will gain some knowledge of the risks that are inherent and those that are hidden. One of the basic things about making stock investments of any kind is to first assess your strategy.

How much risk should I take on and when?

Should I be investing small amounts over long terms or short terms?

What is the reason I want to invest at all?

Do I want to make money like I would make on a job?

Do I want to just drop a large amount of money in once and let it rise for the future?

How do I keep from losing my ass and all

my money as many have done?

How much time do I want to spend learning and gaining confidence in this opportunity?


To define your strategy is the most important thing to do.  Some even will go so far as to say that they only want to work on 10 baggers or more.  Others are quite happy with their investments growing at a better than inflation and better than the bank savings growth.  Some want to just gamble and play.  Whatever your personal reasons may be, going into it with a good understanding and a fair plan will keep your risks to a minimum and your profits looking better by the day.  My friend that has been making a steady 20% plus over the last 20 years has set that actually as his goal.  When he reaches the 20% rise in the stock price over where he bought in then he sells.  That is it.  By this discipline he has kept his losses to an absolute minimum.  I myself take on a little more risk than most people and with the strategies I talk about here manage to stay well on top of my competition.

There are those who are called fundamentalist investors and those who invest according to the stock advisors from whatever place they seem to speak the best to your itchy ears.

There is in the back of this book a glossary with some basic words and their understanding as per this writing. The dictionary may have more to add to their meanings as well. This is not a catch all book. This is a knife that cuts through the HYPE that is constantly broadcast concerning investing in the American markets.

The one hundred year charter for the Federal Reserve System of private banking that has been going on in America since 1913 will come to an end on December 13th 2013 hopefully. Israel recently went to an all electronic currency and there has been talk of the US doing the same. This will really cause chaos in the market place for a while. There will be some big winners and losers as well.

So you had better go out and dig up your

currency and coin stash and get ready to say goodbye to it! I only know that much at the moment. What I see is that this will have the greatest effect on the Black markets. I don't know how long they will give the people to turn in their currency that they hold either. This is probably too why the Banking systems are fighting so hard against ideas like Bit Coin.

I also did hear too that they will flood the market with cheaper than normal interest on all electronic loans as well if the US goes to an all electronic currency. They plan to drop the unemployment rate to well under 4 percent as I understand now. This was talked about by the boys from Oxford as I recall. As it has turned out they didn't have all the low down on the situation. It didn't come off as they had suggested. But Israel instead of the US was the first to jump into an all electronic currency.

## Table of Contents

1

Hype

2

Helium Balloons

Market ups and downs.

3

International Banking

Online Accounts

4

Life Time Holdings

5

What's In A Name?

6

Mis-Information?

7

Good Investment Choices

8

Bad Investment Choices

# 1

## Hype

It is all about hype when you read most stock pages these days. Buy this don't buy that. The hype can be either for a particular stock or fund or against it and that doesn't matter to me, because it is only hype.

So, then what should I buy and why??

Hype is used to guide the money into the stocks that are being pumped and dumped by the movers and shakers so that they can take advantage of unsuspecting market investors on a regular basis.

When you read things like 'The tech play that is better than the next Google.' or 'every one knows this one will go to the top.' 'Why Buffet thinks this is the best stock for 2013'. These are all hype and should be avoided as possible buys by savvy investors or at least waited on till the price comes back down within reasonable means of making a good return on it.

By the time that Wall Street or some others begin to put the spin (hype) on a particular stock it is usually past the possibility of making real bank on it.  Sure it may go up some more and you may make 20 % or so on it but this is not where most truly big gains will happen.  Often Wall street or some of the others that are hyping the stock are already in it and about to pull their profits out.  Believe me there are many pump and dump scams.  When they have spent some money on hype and many more investors have jumped on the roller coaster ride, then the stock will begin to soar to the height that they were wanting for that extra money and will take the last of their profits.  After the big investors have pulled their profits out then the stock will drop quickly down to where they originally bought in or below.  The only reason why people tell about a particular stock is so that others will jump on the band wagon and help push the stocks up higher (price wise).  They only do this so that they can profit more each time.  This is called pumping and dumping.  Penny stocks may have pumps and dumps that last a day or so and Wall Street pumps them sometimes for 6 months or so.  But, all the big boys do this. Every so often they will pull out of a huge number of investments and the whole house of cards will come crashing down and you will hear them blame it on some other reason rather than tell you they pulled their profits. Believe none of what you hear and half of what you see. Anybody can say anything and many will buy everything that is talked about. The market comes down not because there is a crisis in the world. It comes down because of the major investors pulling the majority of the cash (profit) out of it at one time. The market and the indexes work like a helium balloon. Problem is that people are susceptible to hype because of their inherent laziness and desire to hear about some freebee or great unbelievable deal. I will help you here in these pages of Intrigue to make it so that even a lazy person can prosper in the markets. Cool?

There are some advisors that have track records of decency and these often can lead you to some things that may put some bacon on your table. But by and large the tricks are trying to locate the hidden wealth in the market before Wall street finds it and hypes it.

My basic approach to managing my own personal gains in the market has required me to do a lot of research over the years. Finally I have developed a basic set of rules that allow me to pick certain stocks that often outperform many others in the market and most of the ones that get hyped in the market. I have managed to find some stocks that produce more than 200 to 2000 percent and most in about one to two years. Sometimes I even jump out of them when they hit my target selling price that I expect and afterwards will continue to rise even more. But by not being greedy and sticking to my own plan and research I have been saved many a time by jumping just before they go for bottom again.

My personal rules for investing:

Rule No. 1.   Find out who is buying and who is selling the stock I am looking at. Are the major funds buying or selling? Are there any buying, that are buying up huge volumes of shares? Have they been buying steadily over a period of time? Especially look for those who have a track record for buying winners such as Vanguard, Brown and Brown or Blackrock. Some of the largest fund managers often buy well or no one will buy their funds.

Rule No. 2. I get all of my figures and necessary research from my account broker [You would be wise to start an online account with someone like Trade King or Forex]. Look through the market and find the ones with outrageous high P/E, If you check it out and can't figure why the P/E is so high chances are they are whichever person (who works for which ever company) figured the P/E is not wanting others to find this company and are consequently trying to hide a good company to invest in. If there is a high P/E on some accounts like MSN money or Yahoo and I figure a low P/E then you have a possibility of an earnings beater. If it is earning more than their P/E says then that will push the price of the stock up. High P/E says the stock is overvalued. If the company steadily beats earnings estimates then that is the stock to buy. When a growth stock grows faster than the system says then marks it as a possible good opportunity. Only drug company stocks don't follow this method. If the analysts have the P/E wrong then I have a good percentage of chance to make good money on it. If they figure what the company will make wrongly then I will buy it {only though if it also meets my other requirements for good opportunity stock}. This is because people want to find the analysts wrong and they will then push stock price higher. Usually too this is because the company may be growing at a great rate and making good money on its own but not reflected correctly in the P/E. I look for the ones that the analyst have figured wrong and then I will often make good money on them. Slow steady growth beyond the analysts is what everyone wants.

Rule No. 3. Check out the managers of the company to see what kind of track record they have. Read about some of the decisions they make and how these decisions have affected their company. I look to see if the managers own or are selling or buying their own company stocks. If they don't want to buy or are selling then I won't buy either.  CEO or CFO doesn't buy then why should I?  Another great assessment is to look at how the employees are feeling about the company.  Do they buy the stock are they fighting for something that the company has taken from them.  Do they rate the company highly or poorly?

Rule No. 4.    I check on the sales current and future expected increases.  I check on their products they have and especially what kind of future impact I feel they may have in the world market.  Are they a leader in their particular market or do they impact the leaders in the market in a good way?  Royalty begets royalty.

Rule No. 5.    What kind of debt do they have?  How long have they been in debt and what is their debt to asset ratio?  If they have never made a profit then why are they worth my buying?   Except in usage for research or for drug companies the company should be debt free.

Rule No. 6.    How do they treat the shareholders?  Are they diluting the shares (reverse splits like AIG did). They split the shares and gave the stock holders one for every 10 they used to have. Did the company go bankrupt and close and their stock holders lost everything and then later open up again with the same ticker name and everything like GM and AIG both did? If the company does like Wal-Mart has by doubling peoples shares (stock split) every so often then the people make more money overall because for every stock share you are holding you would have two then. This is good.

Rule No. 7. Lastly what have they done on the charts? What was their overall high and when was it and how many times have they gotten that high and can you see a cycle there? Cycle stocks are constant and the best to buy low and sell high. Some retail stocks are this way.

## 2

### Helium Balloons

Market ups and downs.

So many people watch the stock market every day and the ups and downs of the market seem to always say to them, "Whatever you do don't put your money in here." But the old adage buy low sell high is how you truly make your money grow. Buying and selling is one of the oldest ways to make money in the world.

The stock market actually works like a helium balloon. Let's say helium is money and the balloon is the particular stock you are looking at. When the balloon is filling with money (helium) then, the stock price starts going up. When people continue to add more money the stock goes higher and higher with more interested people listening to hype to put more money in and it will continue to send the price soaring to 200 bagger heights. Then the big boys pull out all their moneys and wow just like a huge hole in the side lets all the helium out the balloon will come crashing down. Likewise when small amounts are put in or taken out then the balloon goes erratically up and down. When you consider this anomaly you will often make your purchases more wisely because you are aware of the fact that at some point it will come back to earth (bottom).

The key is to know when to buy what, how long to hold what, and when to sell what. There are definite cycles in the market. These cycles are always related to the big boys pulling profits and going to the next hype or pump and dump. However when the movers and shakers want to pull their profits; which they do at times, most fund owners and brokers are often caught with their pants down and the majority of their customers lose their shirts as sometimes they will as well. Look at how many broker houses failed recently in 2008. How many people lost their life savings? My friends thought of this time as the perfect time for the biggest chances at making huge profits. What happens is that the savvy investors only watch the biggest investors in the world and follow closely where they will put their money. Invariably at some point in time they will pull their profits. You want to get your profits before they take theirs. There are definite ways to know when to do this.

Just as before when we discussed P/E, you must watch your stock page for the changes in P/E and other related information. When you see one of the funds begin to take out some profits or a manager sell off a large number of shares these are definite clues that your time for staying in there may be about to end as well. If your stock it near your selling price then you should consider selling also and especially if it is over your selling price. Now if you see the big boys only pull a little out then you may stay in a while longer if all your figures say that it should go even higher. This is the time to watch the news about your company as well and check on what is happening with them. If for instance they just signed a major agreement and will be selling more products or have gotten a larger quarter earnings showing then you may stay in. On the other hand if something has happened like a hostile takeover or they have lost a contract or a major manager has resigned and sold his portion of stock then it may be time to pull out regardless of where you thought your selling price should have been.

Never buy a stock in November. More than likely it will drop more in December. Almost always it will drop further. Tax sells happen in December. Many people figure how much money will be lost at the end of the year and may even sell at a loss and turn around and buy it again in January to March just to cut their tax rate. Usually this is the big boys that have billions to invest like investment firms and banks. These are the ones who really pump in the helium to those wonderful balloons.

There are what some call pumps and dumps. These are considered illegal. What is true though is that all are actually pumped and at some point when the profit is lucrative enough the big guys dump the load to profit. So buy those that will rise and fall in short periods of time will actually make more money for you as well. But LOW and Sell HIGH! Some will pump and dump in minutes. Others can take years.

Usually it is the Drug companies and the tech companies that will harbor the most exciting and quick bucks for the savvy investor. This will require you to watch them closely and like I said you may buy in and then after a few days it will spike to well over 150 times your original investment or more and then you must jump out immediately as it will fall again in seconds.

3

## International Banking

Online Accounts

The latest in stirring controversy is in Cyprus these days. The government there literally closed the banks and took (some say stole) 6 to 10 percent of all the people's money. Wow!! Unbelievable.

Large banks like Wells Fargo and Co. aren't supposed to be legally able to invest in stocks. Some have investment firms inside the bank that have the same names.

You can today start a banking account from your computer nearly anywhere in the world.

There are many different ways to do it as well. You can transfer funds or wire funds or even send checks in the mail to start accounts with. What you want to be sure of however is whether that country is in need of making amends to the IMF or BIS before you trust their banks with your money.

Today the banks are more and more aligned with one another.  That being said then you can expect to have more and more problems dealing with them.  So, it would behoove any one to stay on top of the changes in laws that are constantly forcing people to stay one jump ahead of them in order to stay safe financially.

Panama, Seychelles, Mauritius, Singapore, Hong Kong, and other countries still maintain some international opportunities.  You should look at whether these opportunities will be good for you now or in the future.  It may depend on how much you plan to make or invest and where those investment and profits will come from and where you are living.  Establishing a trust may be your best option.

Lately the U.S. Government has issued an executive order that allows for the government employees to invade the safety deposit boxes to search for evidence of terrorism. The new NDAA also allows for confiscation of whatever the government feels it may need at any given time also, whether it is land, buildings, or even gold.

The U.S. government is also going after people that are taking major investments out of the U.S. and even the ones who are getting rid of their U.S. passport. You must be careful with the U.S. government and other governments to protect your assets. Hiring a good accounting firm with major experience in your prospective avenue of need is probably not a bad idea. Many countries have now enacted new laws to keep large sums of money from leaving the country without their knowing. Some will not allow cash transactions of more than so much money per day regardless and others will make other laws to control how much is transferred as well.

For those who are looking for information about the broader opportunities for anonymity here you go; http://www.escapeartist.com/Offshore/Asset_Protection/

# 4

## Life Time Holdings

Often when people think of investing in the stock market they will think you invest once and watch your stocks grow and make you money for the rest of your life so that you can retire some day and not have to worry. Today they have a fat purse. But not all companies work quite like that. Were it not for the bad stock advisors and brokers or the big clearing houses pulling their profits all at once maybe just maybe it could be this way. But then you have such market manipulators as Merrill Lynch and those CEOs that put huge volumes into derivatives games that cause whole companies like Enron

 to go belly up. This really hurts everyone who doesn't have billions to lose. Many have been ruefully shamed over these kinds of loses and find it extremely hard to risk being burned in the stock market again. Some however have made considerable amounts of money in the rise of greats like

Wal-Mart WMT: NYSE or some of the Blue chip stocks like General Electric (GE). These stocks can often pay dividends and go through splits and grow over the years and defy the markets up and downs. However, once they have achieved a large price for individual stock share then it is doubly difficult for the small players to make very much on them. These companies typically become huge and therefore have a very large number of outstanding stock shares. When this happens you must have a very large amount of investment capital to invest if you want to make a lot of money off of them. Having the large numbers of shares means that when the prices go up they tend to only go up by very small amounts as it takes a much larger amount of money to impact that many shares. Likewise too if the price per share is already up there like on Google or Amazon then it takes more money to buy large numbers of shares as well. Far better to buy shares when the price is less than 5 dollars apiece and hold them till the price rises to over 50 (10 times your money) or like some when they bought in at just under 10 dollars and the price went up over 300 dollars per share

( 30 times your money). If your investment was $5000 dollars then you would have $50,000 in the first scenario after an appropriate wait and the same $5000 would bring your nest egg to $150,000 in the second. However if you buy in at 100 dollars a share on the second one with 5000 dollars then it would only net you after waiting just $150 dollars to talk about. So this is why you see that it is so important to catch your buys way low and then hope that they rise way high! Investment firms often buy dollar stocks but will tell you that they don't recommend buying under 20 dollars a share.

   Follow the yellow brick road. Some people that have read the financials for years know when Buffet, or some other guru is going to buy something or another but in reality this only talks about one of thousands of decisions that Buffet or whoever may make in a day. Some make money lucratively on Day Trading. But, to avoid penalties in taxes these days it is smart to hold your purchases over the length of at least one year. In this manner you will not be hit so hard by the tax boys from America. They want all your money for sure!

My ex-wife was one of those who did well with Wal-Mart. She got in there when the initial stocks that she purchased were around $20 USD per share and she started with about $10,000. She had a company policy of investing from her paycheck, about $100 USD per week that went into the account for years. Now regardless of where the price was she continued to buy. Most buyers should like I said only buy when the price is low. However because of the continued investment and the fact that Wal-Mart

 had two, two for one splits, she managed to accrue quite a savings from 1995 to today.

5

## What's In A Name?

Stock names are so often a real interesting way to uncover a hit!

In real-estate it is location, but here it can be all in a mane. Names often attract investors for one reason or another. Same goes with the internet and the places that get the most hits amongst the clickers.

Take POT (Potash Corp. of Saskatchewan, Inc.) for instance or IRS (IRSA Investments and Representations Inc.). These are acronyms for things that are highly recognized in the lives of many Americans. Pot is a reference to marijuana a commonly used drug on the streets but as a company symbol on the stock exchange it takes on a whole new light.

The market as well as life these days is full of media beating on us to get us to buy whatever at the moment they are talking about. We get this almost 24/7/365. There doesn't seem to be any getting away from it. In the midst of all of it is the constant nagging of the Wall Street bunch too. They have a new lead on a fat stock that everyone should buy or a question as to whether you want to make millions before your neighbor finds out the one they just told you about along with a billion other people. There is a constant barrage of information and the vast majority of it is just a lot of BS.

There is a manipulation in every one's life. If the name has a nostalgic meaning then it will impact the market as many will recognize that feeling and go with it. Certain names will allow themselves to be hyped and if the company is legit and actually worth buying then it will do greatly. Look at West Point Innovations. It isn't making any money but with a little hype it may go over a hundred dollars a share. First Solar went up over 300 dollars a share and wasn't really much of a good company.

Solar City started out like gang busters and is today considered to be one of the best. These are technology stocks. Sun Power is a California company that is also tied to a German company and is probably doing well because of the ties with their German counterpart. A spin off that has access to the parent companies associations and market opportunities for sales is a great place to often find many small caps that will become 10 baggers. This is also a way that trends will help push certain companies with good names. Techs like these are even called Wall Street darlings. Techs though are sometimes limited by the facts that new techs will come out with new products. Net Flix was a great example. It was down to about 5 at the IPO and when a friend of mine caught it at 16 it went up past 50 where he got out of it and then it finally went all the way up to 300 after about 2 years. Game changers will change things but only for a while till another game changer comes along.

## 6

## Mis-Information?

The market as well as life these days is full of media beating on us to get us to buy whatever at the moment they are talking about. We get this almost 24/7/365. There doesn't seem to be any getting away from it. In the midst of all of it is the constant nagging of the Wall Street bunch too. They have a new lead on a fat stock that everyone should buy or a question as to whether you want to make millions before your neighbor finds out the one they just told you about along with a billion other people. There is a constant barrage of information and the vast majority of it is just a lot of BS.

I have a set theory that I always follow. I don't accept any information unless corroboration is had by more than one witness. My momma always told me to believe none of what you hear and only half of what you see. So, it is like this; if you read something that is coming from one publishing house then you should hear the same from the opposition in some form. In other words if your writers that you read most often are telling you something you think important then you should also find something similar written by writers that you seldom read as well who belong to a totally unrelated source. I often don't make decisions on only two sources either. I will search three or four or more depending on how important a decision I will make on the value of the information.

If you're interested in just making a few extra bucks every couple of years then you can easily do that by using some of the techniques listed here in this book.

Many people will go with what they know and this is the best way to do things, because you will make fewer mistakes and be less fooled by hype and misinformation. Research though is still vital to making quality decisions.

You often should watch how other people push products and therefore companies into trends. The majority of people may not even be aware of these things either. Take for instance the Cell phone market and now the Smart phone market.

It is often known that statistics are subjective. Your own opinion can at times seem to be a fact to you and in your mind you may try to stand on it as if it were a fact. For this very reason many become losers in the investment circles. If you see that your investment has gone sour and that you have taken a loss then (providing it is just not a market manipulation where the big boys are just shorting the hell out of it) then you should get out of it. A stock that is a lemon is one that is actually going bankrupt or is in some other way risking its future and your future with it. Some people have seen 500% drops in their share prices and knowing that the company hasn't changed its modus operandi then and afterwards just hold tight and wait for the helium to fill it again, and NEVER buy a stock in November. More than likely it will drop more in December. Almost always it will drop further. Tax sells happen in December. Many people figure how much money will be lost at the end of the year and may even sell at a loss and turn around and buy it again in January to March just to cut their tax rate. Usually this is the big boys that have billions to invest like investment firms and banks. These are the ones who really pump in the helium to those wonderful balloons.

Load up again since the price is so very low. Then you can really see 2000 to 3000 percent increases. This may often happen in a crashed market and small caps too will have this happen especially if a lawyer is snooping around.

Most of my friends and this is my opinion too; never buy any stock that is over 10 dollars. Depending on their past, they maybe even wait to buy the stock until it falls to under a dollar. You know that if you spend $5000 dollars on a stock at less than a dollar and it goes to only 10 dollars then you have made a good percentage, or $45,000+/-- on a $5000 dollar investment. When you understand the leverage effect of purchasing at a loooowwwww price then you will always look for that opportunity.

Russell Investments on how employees are

doing in different companies.

Forbes has a list of companies rated by employees.

Look through the market and find the ones with outrageous high P/E, If you check it out and can't figure why the P/E is so high chances are they are whichever person (who works for which ever company) figured the P/E is not wanting others to find this company and are consequently trying to hide a good company to invest in.  If there is a high P/E on some accounts like MSN money or Yahoo and I figure a low P/E then you have a possibility of an earnings beater.  If it is earning more than their P/E says then that will push the price of the stock up.  High P/E says the stock is overvalued.  If the company steadily beats earnings estimates then that is the stock to buy.  When a growth stock grows faster than the system says then mark it as a possible good opportunity

# 7

## Good Investment Choices

What makes you money?

Winners and how to mark them and understand them and what they may bring in for your personal gains. Vanguard is a large investment fund which often pumps up stocks that then sell at high profits and then goes and finds another that they want to hype and do it all over again.

Go to Nasdaq.com and check out the various stock tickers.

Stratasy NASDAQ:SSYS, in 2009 they were a 50 million market cap. Their products sell well and this increased their market cap by 2013 to about 1.6 billion market cap. (Often to find accurate information you must go to places like Scott Trade where all the accurate information is available and then you add it up and figure the correct ratios to make good decisions. They won numerous technology awards for high tech invention awards in revolutionary technology.

Latest product award won in 2013 Jan. 28.

New technology they have is a printer that prints 3D parts and even guns.

This will change the way that life will be lived in the future. For a long time Wall Street would hype it down and pushed it down from a 52 week high of about 91 dollars down to near 10 dollars as of Feb. 2013

Often tech stocks will catch a rotation. They will continuously go higher on consecutive rotations till a certain market cap.

Terradata NYSE:TDC

The reason that TDC is doing so good is because it can take a company that is not performing well and turn it into a gold mine. They use software that tells the company how to get the most out of any company and make the right decisions to make higher profits.

Brought China Post into the black because they couldn't keep up with all the tasks they needed to do.

Overstock.com was losing money and didn't ever meet estimates for profits. But with the help of Terradata they are now rising up in the lime life.

Amazon is using it now. Cloud computing has made the better of it.

E-Bay is now making a great comeback.

These are the things to look for when judging whether a company is a viable opportunity to invest in. You can see it in the earnings improvements.

Management is very important to understand where the company will go in the short term and long term.

Check out IRS (IRSA Investments and Representations Inc.). The way that you know a stock is a good one is by watching other large banks and funds and where they will put their money.

NASDAQ:CIMT Cimarron is a company that has produced one of the most exciting inventions in the past few decades if not for the last century. They can print out 3D products and not just on paper. They are an international software company for 3D which is a hot, hot sector now for investments.

When the outstanding shares are very high

in number then the stock is said to be heavy. Heavy companies without sales and only buys will slowly rise but never become a ten bagger.

When the outstanding shares are low in number then the company is said to be light and thus a small amount of sales of share can cause the price to rise rather quickly.

The founder of Baidu and the founder of Apple, both recently have died and those companies went straight down to the nubbins. But both companies are poised for a return providing they can find decent replacements that the shareholders will put their faith into again.

These are some stocks that, as of the printing of this book, my friends and I think highly of:

Transcat Inc.  TRNS  $6.17

52wk Range:    4.97 - 8.55The Female Health Company   FHCO  $8.27

52wk Range: 5.25 - 8.39 Inter Digital Inc. IDCC $47.19

52wk Range: 22.37 - 48.68 The Medicines Company MDCO $36.73

52wk Range: 20.04 - 37.40
Aegion Corporation AEGN $22.65

52wk Range: 14.49 - 26.10 Nature's Sunshine Products Inc. NATR $14.83

52wk Range: 12.91 - 18.39 iRobot Corporation IRBT $34.51

52wk Range: 16.25 - 34.94 Intuitive Surgical, Inc. ISRG $484.40

52wk Range: 455.18 - 585.67 Sun Hydraulics Corp. SNHY $32.35

52wk Range: 20.81 - 34.22

Neogen Corp. NEOG $54.05

52wk Range: 37.26 - 54.86Stratasys Ltd. SSYS $90.90

52wk Range: 42.71 - 94.9

CBIZ, Inc. CBZ $6.64

52wk Range: 5.07 - 6.65KCAP Financial, Inc. KCAP $11.19

52wk Range: 5.51 - 11.38Telular Corporation WRLS $12.69

52wk Range: 7.05 - 13.01EPIQ

Express Scripts Holding Company ESRX $61.38

52wk Range: 49.79 - 66.06Teradata Corporation TDC $54.27

52wk Range:     48.81 - 80.97

51job Inc.  JOBS  $58.04

52wk Range:     34.00 - 61.74Rochester Medical Corporation  ROCM  $14.73

52wk Range:     9.11 - 15.34

MarketAxess Holdings Inc.  MKTX  $45.77

52wk Range:     26.14 - 46.29

I must say again. Some of these at the writing are up in price above where I typically will invest. I only personally like to invest when the stocks are below $5.00 USD. Preferably down around a dollar is where I like to jump into the battle. The odds are that if I do pick a winner there then the winnings will be much more substantial. If I pick a loser then I have not lost a hell of a lot.

Recently a friend of mine has taken an investment of only 5000 and in six months turned into more than 75,000. He did this by staying up and watching the market like a hawk for those that will spike in just a few minutes and then drop like a rock.

Here is where you need to find the real deal. This following list below is where I have often found fairly decent advice. There are many such companies;

Insider Monkey   .....
 http://www.insidermonkey.com

This site, Insider Monkey, is a key site for education and watching for movements in the other companies that are actively trading day to day. Often you find exceptional informative article here to help with your understanding of the market and making quality decisions on investments.

Business Insider Money Game   ......
 http://www.bussinessinsider.com

Motley Fool   .....   http://www.fool.com

Gold and Silver   ......

http://www.goldsilver.com

Global Wealth Protection .....
https://www.globalwealthprotection.com

Escape Artist Magazine .......
http://www.escapeartist.com

Penny Stocks .....
http://www.pennystocks.com

Perfect Penny Stocks .....
http://perfectpennystocks.com

Kapital ..... http://wire.kapitall.com

Outsider Club .....
http://outsiderclub.com

Quick and easy quotes are often found on MSN or Yahoo finance pages.

# 8

## Bad Investment Choices

How about AIG and GM?

Look for dilution of shares. Diluted weighted average shares. When they sell off shares to increase earnings then this always brings the equity of other shareholders stock in the company down sometimes to nothing. If the company over a period of years never dilutes the shares then it is living off its income from products and services and will rise in the future. The people in the market place will watch these things more closely these days than in the past as there are more people from other countries that are investing in the NYSE and other exchanges internationally. The modern investor is wiser today.

Often companies from China are purposely shorted to the ground as they are perceived to be not transparent in their activities and accounting by the majority of investors.

However there are some companies with long track records that will rise above this perception and be good opportunities for making cash. From their initial openings they usually will go up so that some can profit initially and then they will be shot to the ground till sometimes they must give up their seat completely. I think that in the future though there will always be some viable contenders from every nation on the exchanges in America.

Lawyers are all around the situations today and they will say all sorts of things that some companies supposedly have done things to steal the people's money. All stocks go up and down. That is the nature of the beast. Where stocks can work against the shareholders, is when there are huge companies that will hype it up and people will jump in too late and then have the rug pulled out from under them by those who have billions invested as they pull their profits.

The founder of the company and the CEO are the ones to watch so as to know whether a company is worth buying into. Such as recently when Steve Jobs died and

Apple stocks fell a long way in price. Quarterly earnings fell as well. When CEO's are under fire by lawyers or when they are negatively presented in the media this too can bring the prices down or make the particular stock in my estimation not a good purchase opportunity.

DISCLAIMER

AS WITH ANY THING WHEN IT COMES TO THE MARKET IN AMERICA THESE DAYS THERE ARE ALWAYS THOSE WHO TRY TO TAKE UNDUE ADVANTAGE. WHAT I HAVE DONE WITH THIS BOOK IS TO GIVE YOU MY OPINION ON THE MATTERS ENCLOSED. IF YOU DO ACT ON ANY OF THESE IDEAS THEN YOU DO SO ON YOUR OWN ACCORD AND AT YOUR OWN PERIL. PLEASE DO YOUR DUE DILIGENCE AND STUDY THE SITUATION BEFORE YOU MAKE ANY INVESTMENTS. IF YOU DON'T, YOU WILL LOSE YOUR MONEY.

I AS WELL AS ANY WHO HAVE WORKED OR HELPED ON THIS BOOK CANNOT BE HELD RESPONSIBLE IF YOU LOSE ANY MONEY. NEITHER I NOR ANY OTHER CONCERNING THIS PUBLICATION CAN BE HELD LIABLE FOR ANY DECISIONS THAT ANY READERS MAY MAKE CONCERNING THE INFORMATION CONTAINED HEREIN.

Thanks for taking the time to read this. If you think that it is worthy at all please let others know by writing a review.

I appreciate it greatly.

--Oz



My web presence;

http://www.love2liveway.com

http://www.smileadz.com

www.ingramcontent.com/pod-product-compliance
Lightning Source LLC
Chambersburg PA
CBHW040922180526
45159CB00002BA/568